Released From Yesterday

Reginald Bynes

ISBN: 978-1-105-08193-4

RELEASED FROM YESTERDAY

© Copyright 2011 – Reginald Bynes

ISBN: 978-1-105-08193-4

All rights reserved. This book is protected by the copyright laws of the United States of America. This book may not be copied or reprinted for commercial gain or profit. The use of short quotations or occasional page copying for personal or group study is permitted and encouraged. Permission will be granted upon request.

Bethel Covenant Worship Center
3958-F Wrightsboro Road
Augusta, GA 30909

Pastor Reginald Bynes
And
First Lady Cynthia Bynes

8th Ed

Dedicated

This book is dedicated to my loving wife Cynthia who has stood with me in ministry and in life. I thank God for her unwavering support. Thank you for your prayers and Godly insight through the process of writing this book.

This book is dedicated to my two daughters Regina and Sophia. I don't know if I could have been blessed with any better daughters. I thank you for support in the ministry and it is my prayer that God will continue to increase you both.

This book is dedicated to my Spiritual father Bishop Eddie L. Long. Thank you for your support and encouragement to take a leap of faith and trust that God was doing the choosing. It was because of your guidance and leadership that I had the courage to write this book. I am forever grateful to you.

And to Dr. Joseph Chandler, I thank you for the help that you gave to me to push through this third "Spiritual" trimester of getting the book done. You did a great job and I thank God for your words of wisdom.

This book is dedicated to those people who have wondered if it is true that God has forgiven you and if He can still use you.

This book is designed to make you think and apply the principles of God's word to your life through faith in Him.

It is for those people who have had trouble getting past things.

It is for those people who have had difficulty accepting the Grace and Mercy of God

It is for those people who have listened to the voices of your past but are willing to listen to the Word of your Present.

It is for anyone who will have problems with moving on and need help and a kick of knowledge.

It is for those who have difficulty smiling, and don't know that God sent Jesus the Christ to pay a price for you to be able to smile.

After reading this book, I know that if you will receive it,

Your confession for tomorrow will change by what you believe today because of what God has released you from on YESTERDAY.

CONTENTS

FIRST WORDS

BABY STEPS

DAY OF DETERMINATION

DON'T YOU DARE SETTLE

FREE IS FREE

GET OUT OF THOSE GRAVE CLOTHES

GETTING PAST THE MUD

I NEVER HELD IT AGAINST YOU

INTERNAL VERSUS EXTERNAL

IT AIN'T THAT BAD

LAUGHING IS AN ART THAT IS LEARNED

MAKE A PLAN

ONLY SLIGHTLY DAMAGED

OPPORTUNITY OF A LIFETIME

OUT TO IN MENTALITY

WILL TO SEPARATE

HEALING POWER OF THE WORD

ARE YOU HERE TO DEMOTE OR PROMOTE

ARE YOU FIT FOR THE ASSIGNMENT

FINAL WORD

FIRST WORDS

It is a true saying that you never get a second chance to make a first impression.

Those are called starting words. The words that we start with will set the pace for what we end up with.

Knowing this, if we begin our days with this thought we would end up with a better perspective on life.

We will get to the point that if our day is important to us, we will take note of the first thoughts that come to our minds knowing that those thoughts can affect our entire day. This is all a building process. We build on those things that will make us better day by day and move forward. If we walk and live in that attitude our every day will be better than our yesterday.

In this book you will see that Jesus spoke to this very same subject.

He came to this world for a purpose and that was to make our day better than Yesterday. And to release us from the bondage of Yesterday

(John 10:10 KJV) "The thief cometh not, but for to steal, and to kill, and to destroy: I am come that they might have life, and that they might have it more abundantly."

If in my day I am given more knowledge, I should be better than yesterday. If in my day I am given a better perspective in life, I should be better than yesterday.

If in my day I am given more of anything, I should be better than yesterday.

BABY STEPS

Just as a babe does not learn to walk all at once, but by gradual steps

You will have to learn how not to be pinned down by your yesterday.

The first thing that you will have to do is make a commitment to yourself to make the attempt to do better in your walking.

Second thing is to stay with it.

You cannot commit to others and help anybody unless you have made the commitment for yourself first.

In Mark 12:30-31 KJV, Jesus said, **"And thou shalt love the Lord thy God with all thy heart, and with all thy soul, and with all thy mind, and with all thy strength: this is the first commandment. And the second is like, namely this, Thou shalt love thy neighbour as thyself. There is none other commandment greater than these."**

"Love your neighbor as yourself"

You can't love others if you don't love yourself first.

It all starts like a baby taking first steps.

There are first steps in moving away from your yesterday.

You will never move away until you make that first step.

The journey of a thousand miles begins with one step.

You may not be able to see down the road but you need to concentrate on what is directly in front of you.

Knowing that in your walking, God has already been where He is telling you to go.

One day at a time is a true saying.

Baby steps are careful steps. When you commit to take baby steps don't get discourage because you have a long way to go.

Be encouraged when you look and see how far you have come.

Even as a child stumbles, the child does not give up because of a stumble.

Don't give up, encourage yourself and say to yourself, I am committed to making this walk in life work for me.

If you are committed to take a look at every step that you make, your focus will be on how you are walking.

(Eph 5:15 KJV) "See then that ye walk circumspectly, not as fools, but as wise"

God knows that you are taking baby steps because He is the one walking behind you to make sure that you don't fail. (Not fall) but not fail.

Change your eye sight:

The process, power, or function of seeing or the ability to see

I want to deal with the word ability.

In the scriptures when we see the word Power when Jesus was talking to the disciples, He would often refer to power.

The power that Jesus is referring to is ability to accomplish something.

Every one of us has been given the ability to see or the power to see.

We have to be willing to look and recognize what it is that we see.

We often look at each other in terms of relationships and the relationship is based on how we "see" the other person.

That is called natural or carnal.

God does not see us in the same light. He sees us as He has ordained us.

The reason God sees us as He ordained us is that God is not looking at where you are or what you have done. He is looking at what He has called you to.

And in everything that God has called us to, is our purpose in life.

We see each other as we are; with problems, with flaws, with cracks, with failures, with disappointments and the list goes on and on.

God see us as His plan.

(Jeremiah 29:11 NIV) "For I know the plans I have for you," declares the LORD, "plans to prosper you and not to harm you, plans to give you hope and a future."

When we begin to see each other as God sees us, we will in turn start to see ourselves as God sees us.

The blockage in our life is not always the other person. The blockage is sometimes us.

We let what happened block us from seeing what is.

(Rom 4:17 KJV) "(As it is written, I have made thee a father of many nations,) before him whom he believed, even God, who quickeneth the dead, and calleth those things which be not as though they were."

When we start to call others what God has already called them, we begin our own road to healing.

We need to see each other in the state that God sees us.

It will point to what kind of heart we have and what kind of intention we have.

This will not happen until we change our sight.

Our spiritual sight can lead us to greater vision than our natural sight.

Our spiritual sight can lead us into places our natural sight cannot take us.

It will become a cause in your life.

God has already seen you and me. And even though He has seen you and me,
God did not change his mind after He saw us.

He saw us as we were and called us as He had ordained us.

How can that be? I am glad you asked that.

(Isaiah 55:8 KJV) "For my thoughts are not your thoughts, neither are your ways my ways, saith the LORD."

(Isaiah 55:9 KJV) "For as the heavens are higher than the earth, so are my ways higher than your ways, and my thoughts than your thoughts."

When we come to the point in our lives that we are willing to change our thoughts and start to think like God, our sight in life will start to change.

We will stop seeing as we see and see things as God has ordained them.

DAY OF DETERMINATION

You have the ability and the right to determine what kind of day you are going to have.

You decide all of this the moment that you wake up.

The first thought will be the one thing that will guide you through your day.

If you wake up with a determination in your mind that you are going to have a good day, YOU will.

And the opposite of that is also true.

My past is an indicator of just how good of a life that I have now! My now will give me hope for a better tomorrow.

Start today and get determined to get better

Start today and get determined to do better

Start today and get determined to think better

Start today and get determined to act better

Start today and get determined to live better

Start today and get determined to be better

It is a choice that God gives you on a daily basis

(2 Corinthians 4:16 KJV) "For which cause we faint not; but though our outward man perish, yet the inward man is renewed day by day."

DON'T YOU DARE SETTLE!

In life when we have certain problems in our life and we don't know that we have options we will settle.

In all of what we settle for, we get less than what we want.

God never intended for us to settle for anything in life.

God expects for us to come out on top every time and in every situation

(1 Corinthians 15:57 KJV) "But thanks be to God, which giveth us the victory through our Lord Jesus Christ."

That means that God has already done the fighting for you and brought the victory and gave it to you. You did not have to lift a finger to get it, **IT IS A GIVEN.**

Let's take a quick look in the Bible

John chapter 11

We all know the story of Lazarus coming out of the tomb.

But there is another story line there.

There were two sisters, one named Mary and the other Martha.

The bible says that they sent word for Jesus to come and heal their brother.

Jesus did not come right away and their brother died.

The story turns and tells more of the two sisters.

(John 11:20 KJV) "Then Martha, as soon as she heard that Jesus was coming, went and met him: but Mary sat still in the house."

The two sisters both said the same thing to Jesus "If you had been here our brother would not have died. "

But Martha qualified her statement with a statement of facts and faith.

Mary just said if you had been here our brother would not have died.
Martha said if you had been here our brother would not have died.

BUT, I know.....

BUT I know something else.

Mary settles for the fact that after she had requested for Jesus to come and He did not, her brother died.

Martha did not settle for what she had been given.

Martha came to a point in her life called the **"EVEN NOW"** point.

She stated even though my brother is dead.

I believe that even now, he can live.

Even though it looks bad, it sounds bad, it feels bad,

EVEN NOW

Whatever you ask God, He will give it to you.

If it worked for Martha, it will work for you

All you have to do is, have the <u>faith</u> to ASK !
Don't you dare settle for what you see.
Believe God for those things that you don't see and don't understand.

FREE IS FREE

When you come to the point in your life that you really understand what it means to be free, you are at the point where you no longer can be bound by anybody or anything.

Free means just what it says.

If you have to pay for it

It is not free.

The word free will create a separation in your life that will not allow you to be consumed by the opinions of others.

(John 8:36 KJV)" If the Son therefore shall make you free, ye shall be free indeed."

Jesus wanted us to be free in every area of our lives.

(Gal 5:1 KJV) "Stand fast therefore in the liberty wherewith Christ hath made us free, and be not entangled again with the yoke of bondage."

It is vital that you understand that freedom is the exact opposite of bondage.

For whom the Son has set free is free indeed.

That means that you have been separated from bondage and given the freedom to do and become who God intended for you to be.

If you need a picture of freedom, just talk to anybody who used to be in bondage.

GET OUT OF THOSE GRAVE CLOTHES

We have to understand how important it is to our mind that we get out of the grave clothes in order to get into our destiny.

What are grave clothes? They are the things or people in life that will hang onto you and prevent you from moving forward in life.

Graves's clothes are those things that will prevent you from seeing what God has said concerning your life.

Notice that there a passage of scripture in the book of Matthew Chapter 28

That says that when those people who went to the tomb of Christ expecting to see his body, suddenly discovered and was informed by an angel that He was not there.
The beautiful thing is that, they were invited into the tomb for two reasons.

(Matthew 28:6 KJV) "He is not here: for he is risen, as he said. Come, see the place where the Lord lay."

1- To be witnesses that Jesus was not in the tomb, that He had done what He had promised by getting up on the third day.
2- To see what was left in the grave.

Jesus got up and left everything in the grave that was not like Him.

He left **everything** that wanted to hang on to him. He left everything that said death and not life.

We find ourselves in the same condition of life sometimes. But we have to be willing to leave some things in the tomb in order to move forward.

We find things hanging on us and preventing us from moving forward in the thing that God has ordained for our life.

They are not physical grave clothes, they are the clothes of life that hang on and tend to keep us back.

Some of us have old memories that will prevent us from moving forward.

Some of us have un-forgiveness that prevents us from moving forward.

Some of us have negative thoughts of our life and that will prevent us from moving forward.

Some of us have in-decisions and that will prevent us from moving forward.

Some of us are full of fear and that will prevent us from moving forward.

With all of that, if we would just understand that we have the power to leave some things in the tomb we can move forward.

If you can just make up your mind that today is the last day that grave clothes are going to dominate your life, you can step into what God has ordained for your life.

When Jesus stepped out of the grave and left the grave clothes, He stepped into the next phase of His ministry.

When you step out of what's been holding you back, you will step into another dimension of the Glory of God and the purpose of God in your life.

Don't wait another day, Drop the grave clothes and step…

Drop the grave clothes and step into…

Drop the grave clothes and watch God perform wonders in your life…

Drop the grave clothes and watch God…

Drop the grave clothes and watch what God can do in you and through you…

You have to step out before you can step in.

Step out and **leave** everything that is not like God in the grave.

Don't drag it out with you, leave it in the grave.

If there were things that Jesus could leave in His grave,

You have the power to leave your things in your grave.

GETTING PAST THE MUD

OFTEN TIMES IN OUR LIVES WE COME TO A POINT WHEN WE HAVE TO HAVE MUD PUT ON US.

We see for cosmetic purposes that people don't mind bathing and smearing mud on them to get a therapeutic effect on their bodies.

We go to great lengths to do that. We will travel to exotic places and pay large sums of money just to have a few minutes of relief.

And we find ourselves saying *"It was worth the time, effort, and expense to have a few minutes or hours that were produced from that one outing."*

I often look at travel shows that explain the importance of a mud lava makeover. Nobody seems to mind that they are having mud placed on them and dipping them into a tub of mud. It is great because they expect a result from allowing themselves to be smeared with mud.

Jesus understood that in the book of John chapter 9. He met a man who had a need in his physical body and Jesus understood that mud would and could being mixed with the Godly authority that was in Him, produced a desired effect that a blind man had.

God's word is always therapeutic. Most would say that I am not going to have mud put on me because it is dirt. The mud was only the tool that would produce healing in the life of a blind man. Had this blind man not submitted to having the mud smeared on him, he would not have gotten the desire effect *(the ability to see)*.

This blind man had to get beyond having mud put on him. The mud was necessary to his healing.

God's word is like mud. It has a power to heal, deliver and set free.

But it will not do you any good unless you submit to the smearing affect.

The blind man was healed not just because of the mud but he was healed because he was willing to do and follow the instructions that would lead to his healing.

(John 9:11 KJV) "He answered and said, A man that is called Jesus made clay, and anointed mine eyes, and said unto me, Go to the pool of Siloam, and wash: and I went and washed, and I received sight."

It was the three things combined that got him healed.

1- He requested healing
2- He submitted to having mud on him

3- He was told to go and wash in a pool called Siloam *(which means Sent)*

It was these three things combined that got him healed.

When he submitted, it opened him up to something and a world that he had never seen before. He was no longer dependent on people having to lead him around. He now had the capacity to walk and not wait to be led.

God wants to do the same for each one of us. Your only dilemma is the question; can you get past the mud? The mud is the technique that will get you to your healing.

Can you get past the mud?

The word, **"anoint"** in verse 11 means to smear. When he allowed himself to be smeared with the mud, his eyes were opened as a result of following the instructions. If he had not <u>allowed</u> the Lord to "smear" him, he would not have gained his sight.

God only wants you smear you so that you can gain sight, not lose your way.

If you have been smeared before by others, allow the Lord to smear you with his love.

Allow Him to smear you with his wisdom.

Allow Him to smear you with who He is.

I guarantee that you will be healed.

Take a note of this history. **"Everybody that Jesus laid hands on was healed."**

Let him lay hands on you in your heart and He will heal everything that is in your life that needs healing.

It may seem like mud. But if you can get past what it looks like, you can get on with your healing.

I NEVER HELD IT AGAINST YOU

We often times think that God thinks the way that we think. That is the one thing that is the farthest from the truth.

(Isaiah 55:8 KJV) "For my thoughts are not your thoughts, neither are your ways my ways, saith the LORD."

I remember some years ago that I had gotten to a place where I did not want anyone or God to tell me what to do. I had my own spiritual rebellion. During this time, in my own narrow way of thinking, I thought that I and God would have it out and I would go my way and He would go his way.

I told God to leave me alone concerning my assignment and get somebody else to do it. I shook my fist at Him and said **"I DON"T WANT IT!"**

Now in the natural when someone goes to that degree to tell you that they want no part of you, we would let them go.

God's way was not to let me go. I later understood why.

I came upon,

(Jeremiah 1:5 KJV) "Before I formed thee in the belly I knew thee; and before thou camest forth out of the womb I sanctified thee, and I ordained thee a prophet unto the nations."

Little did I know that God had already invested in me and that He was not giving up on His investment. I hope that this is helping somebody today. You are not an accident, you are not a mistake, and you are not what they say you are. You are the investment of God and He is not giving up on you.

I later in this story came to a point where I had a Spirit Filled moment with God one day in church.

All of the things that I had said in frustration, came back to my remembrance one day in a church meeting that I had no plans of being involved in that day.

God turned the situation around and the ones, who I thought God was speaking to, were not the ones, who God spoke to that day.

I ended up being cornered by the Holy Spirit and had nowhere to run and nowhere to hide.

I knew that I was caught and I knew what was coming next. All of a sudden I could not stand up straight.

I was bent over at the knees, standing at the altar and holding on to the last bit of strength that I had.

When God began to speak to me, I braced myself for the punishment that was to follow. As a child knows when their parent is about to correct them, I knew that God was about correct me with a spiritual beat down. I cringed and braced for a whacking from God.

It was at that moment that I heard a voice in a gentle tone that said,

"I never held it against you".

In all of your rebellion "I never held it against you".

In all of your self-centeredness "I never held it against you".

That small voice broke me down to a point that I had never seen or heard in my life.

Little did I know that I was at my point of spiritual restoration.

It was in that quick moment that God restored and made me understand what is meant in the prayer of the disciples, "Our Father, which art in heaven". And He is Our Father, the one who covers us.

The Spirit of God came up to me and spoke very softly in the ear of my understanding and said,

"I NEVER HELD IT AGAINST YOU".

Then in all the power that I had braced, I broke down and wept. It was the greatest weeping of my life.

It freed me to hear more of God. He then said. Now go do what I have called you to do.

I knew then that God had made an investment in my life, I am determined that He gets;

A good return for His investment!
No matter who you are and what you have done and what they have told you.

God says to you today and let this be a word in the Spirit that will free you to do what He has ordained for your life

I NEVER HELD IT AGAINST YOU. NOW GO DO WHAT I HAVE CALLED YOU TO DO.

INTERNAL VERSUS EXTERNAL

This is a very good look at how God deals with us and how he sees us.

He does not deal with us as other men do but, He deals with us according to his divine nature.

(Isaiah 55:8 KJV) "For my thoughts are not your thoughts, neither are your ways my ways, saith the LORD."

(Isaiah 55:9 KJV) "For as the heavens are higher than the earth, so are my ways higher than your ways, and my thoughts than your thoughts."

There is an internal influence in all of us and an external influence.

We often will work on us from the outside and take care of the inside later.

Let me give you a good example.

We get up in the morning and go through our daily routine of making us look good.

We groom and put on make-up and the clothing that says to people who see us.

(They must be doing well)

We wear our perceptions and appearances for others to get a view that may not be true.

We work hard at making us look good to others without taking the time to make sure that we are looking good on the inside.

If we take the same time that we take to make the outside look good, and apply it to our inside we would be better off.

But this is the human side of us. Man looks on the external but God deals with the internal first.

Why, because if we get the inside right, the outside will have conform to the inside.

There is a story in the Book of Mark chapter two where a man had palsy. He went to see Jesus in order to get healed. After all the trouble they went through to get to Jesus, he did not get what he wanted right away.

(Mark 2:5 KJV) "When Jesus saw their faith, he said unto the sick of the palsy, Son, thy sins be forgiven thee".

Why did Jesus do this? Because the important part of this man was not in his physical state. He needed to work on him from the inside first. When he allowed the Lord to work on his inside, the outside was automatically taken care of.

The same will go for you if you allow the Lord to work on you internally first, the external will always conform to the internal.
This is the reason you will find a person who is always happy and upbeat. The inside has been taken care of and the outside which is what you see has conformed to the inside.

Start today and make a change and tell God I submit to you to work on me internally in order to affect my external. Try it, it really does work and will set you on a path to seeing yourself better than yesterday.

IT AIN'T THAT BAD

We all have had times in our lives where we have been in the position where we thought that it could not get any worse than this and I am at the end of my life.

I remember as a young man growing up, how we used to play and end up getting cut or hurt while playing.

When we were cut, we would always turn away from the cut because we had already developed a picture in our mind of just how bad the cut was.

The mental picture formed because of what we thought before we saw anything.

The mental picture is always formed from what we remember from past experience and what we have heard of others.

We develop hurt feelings in the same manner. We will not look at the situation but, we have a mental picture that is already formed without the evidence to back up what we think. The key word here is the word "think". This is like a person who has or thought they saw a ghost. There is no evidence of what we thought. It is full of what we thought.

Your thought process is the key. Whys is that so? It is so because what you think does matter.

"As a man thinks in his heart so is he" Proverbs 23:7

And what you think will shape your attitude.

It will shape your life in every area. It will lay a foundation for who you are and who you can become. Attitude is so important that God himself measures a man by his attitude.

(Zephaniah 2:3 NIV) "Seek the LORD, all you humble of the land, you who do what he commands. Seek righteousness, seek humility; perhaps you will be sheltered on the day of the Lord's anger."

Even the Prophet Daniel had to have a good attitude before he was given much.

It was in his attitude that he was promoted. The right spirit will promote you to great things in life. It is not because of what you have attained or obtained. It is the attitude in which you do it.

(Dan 6:3 KJV) "Then this Daniel was preferred above the presidents and princes, because an excellent spirit was in him; and the king thought to set him over the whole realm."

Notice here that for no other reason but that Daniel was found to be faithful and had an excellent spirit.

Write this down and tell it to yourself over and over again.

During the tough times tell it to yourself;

"A good attitude and excellent spirit will get you far"

Tell it to yourself over and over.

You will find out that your tomorrow will be better than yesterday if you face your today with a mindset that I am going to have an excellent spirit about me today and everything that I do. If you get to that point you can turn around any situation because you now have a positive attitude toward your day to day life.

Now think…………..about what it is that is so troubling you.

Look and listen to your heart of the matter.

Think about how long it has been since you started with it.

Think about how much it has hurt you.

Think about how long you have allowed yourself to hurt from it.

Think about how much time you have spent thinking on it.

Think about how much labor you have put into it.

Now, think about how your heart has survived this long.

Now, think about how long you have survived it.

Now, think about how much the hurt has occupied your life.

Now, think about how much time you have had to heal from it.

Now, think about the fruit of your labor in it.

You have been blessed through all of it.

It did not ultimately consume you.

It did not take you off of the deep end.

You have made it and now look in the mirror.

Not the mirror of your mind your real mirror and tell yourself you look good.

You WERE hurt but you made it.

You were mad, but you discovered that it is not worth your life to stay mad.

You WERE angry but you discovered that anger didn't change it.

If you realize all of those things, you can look BACK over your life and the entire situation and say,

IT AINT THAT BAD!

Selah……..

LAUGHING IS AN ART THAT IS LEARNED

You need to learn how to laugh.

In this life if you do not learn how to laugh,

You will not last.

(Proverbs 17:22 KJV) "A merry heart doeth good like a medicine: but a broken spirit drieth the bones."

The reason I say that this is something that you learn is because,

Everybody does not have the ability to laugh.

It is available to everyone but everyone does not use that tool of life to their benefit.

Nobody can make you laugh; you have to choose to laugh.

Process that thought, and decide if you are willing to look at it and just **LAUGH**.

You have the ability to change your day.

You have the ability to change your despair into hope.

You have the ability to change your sorrow into joy.

The ability to laugh was given to us by God and if I were you, I would not allow, anybody or anything to take from me the free gift called laughter.

Laughter is one of the greatest mood changers in our life.

If you can make yourself just laugh one time, it will change your mood.

Bad and negative thoughts will keep you in sorrow and depression.

Laughter will be the door that leads you out of every low place.

If you don't believe it, just remember this the next time negative comes your way.

Start laughing and watch negative get upset with you laughing.

Negative thoughts, Negative people, Negative actions, Negative words are all a part of a meal that will not work unless you allow it.

Negativity is a dish that will only be eaten by you if you allow it.

You have to be willing to eat negativity.

Can I take your Order Please!!!!!!!!!

MAKE A PLAN

You have to plan your day.

You have to plan your week.

You have to plan your life.

You have to plan to succeed.

You have to plan to make peace.

You have to plan to get better.

You have to do all of these things before you can attempt to do any of these by others.

By focusing on where you are and making a plan to improve in the areas that you have identified in your life.

A good plan will give you hope.

A Godly plan will move you away from yesterday.

(Phil 3:14 KJV) "I press toward the mark for the prize of the high calling of God in Christ Jesus."

Sometimes you have to go old school and go back to old songs, Roberta Flack, had a song that says;

"The closer I get to you"

The song is talking about a plan.

Getting closer to the Lord will give you confidence.

Getting close to the Lord will make you feel and understand your worth in life.

Getting closer to the Lord will make you give all that you have to get closer.

This is a plan that works!!!

It speaks of a lover who gets closer to their lover and it improves their life.

Make sure that the plan you make has a design on it and in it to make you better.

You have to sit down and Selah (ponder) think about, consider, take thought to.

How happy you want to be.

And then move in the direction of your happiness.

Then build your life's plan around the **good things that you desire**. That thought of betterment will have to be built by you.

Plan- to come out of debt…

Plan to come out of poverty…

Plan to come out of lack…

Plan to come out of whatever is causing you to be unhappy and unfulfilled.

You have to plan a successful prison break for "your mind".

If you don't make a plan, you will not do it.

If you don't make a plan, you do not have anything to work and look forward to.

Plan your positive movements forward and watch the negative thoughts of your yesterday fall away.

Amen.   This was good for me!!!

ONLY SLIGHTLY DAMAGED

You have to look at yourself in the mirror and see that you are still here.

God has brought you through a lot and you are still here.

Understanding in the end that you are at the end of the process and only slightly damage

Not counted out

But only slightly

Not Destroyed, but …

I had a friend when I was growing up. We were always together. When you saw one, you would always see the other. When one bicycle broke down we would both ride the one bike that was still working. One day we decided to go to the local park. And we headed toward the swing set to get on the swings. There was only one swing available.

We both looked at the swing and took off running toward the one swing. I beat my friend to the swing and begin to enjoy the swing. After a short period of time I decided to let my friend have the swing. During this time I did not know what my friend was thinking in his mind. I didn't know that he got upset with me over the swing. I jumped out of the swing to let him have it. As I turned to allow him to have the swing, I felt a stinging and burning feeling on my wrist. I remembered looking out of the corner of my eye to see my friend wind up like a baseball pitcher.

He had gotten a piece of glass and threw it at me and it hit me on the wrist. I looked at him with blood running down my arm and being startled, I asked him, why you did such a thing being that we were supposed to be the best of friends. He never said a word. I said all of that to make this point. I still have the scar on my wrist. Every time I run my hand down my wrist, I can feel that scar from years ago.

The one thing about the scar that my friend gave me years ago is that it does not hurt anymore. I have the scar and not the hurt. I allowed God to heal me of the hurt. When we allow God to heal us, He removes the hurt.

You may have scars but, you are still here. You may have scars but you are only slightly damaged. We need to understand that scars are not a reminder of the one who hurt us.

Your scars are a reminder of the hurt and harm from which God has delivered you.

OPPORTUNITY OF A LIFETIME

We often in life will look back on our failure and judge ourselves when God does not judge us by failure but, by opportunities

(Galatians 6:10 KJV) "**As we have therefore opportunity, let us do good unto all men, especially unto them who are of the household of faith.**"

God has already informed us that He is going to give us opportunities and that they are coming. He then tells us how to or what to do with them.

Our responsibility in the opportunity is that we do well with them. Oftentimes our biggest obstacle is the issue and not the answer.

Opportunities are a result of the plan of God for our life.

(Jeremiah 29:11 NIV) "For I know the plans I have for you," declares the LORD, "plans to prosper you and not to harm you, plans to give you hope and a future."

God says that He knows some things that we don't know.

He has a plan. A plan is always an opportunity. An opportunity is a set of circumstances designed to give you the advantage.

So it is the intent of God operating in your life to give you the upper hand in every area of your life.

In the book of Joshua, God comes to Joshua and tells him that Moses was dead and then immediately turned His attention to the assignment of Joshua. In the natural that may seem a bit insensitive. But in the Spirit realm we need to understand that God's heart was for the Children of Israel. And out of His concern for His children, He turned to Joshua and said, take up the assignment of Moses and lead the people into the promise.

God did not want His people to go without a spokesman. This was an opportunity of a lifetime and the decision that Joshua made at that moment brought him into a covenant with God.

In Joshua 1:5, God said that when Joshua had completed his assignment to take the people over to the Jordan to the promise. He told Joshua that if you do what I command then I will be with you Joshua all the days of your life and "No man "will be able to withstand you all the days of your life. The entire time that Joshua was leader of Israel, there was not one enemy that could overpower the nation, because of the decision that Joshua made to trust and obey God.

We have the same opportunity of a lifetime when we obey God.

(John 15:7 KJV) "If ye abide in me, and my words abide in you, ye shall ask what ye will, and it shall be done unto you."

Just walk out the plan for your life. And watch God operate for you.
He has already promised that "I will never leave you nor forsake you".

They may not like you. They may not be able to stand you. God is saying it does not matter what their opinion is …
Because He is working for you, they won't have the ability to overpower you.
NOW, given that information, you need to wake up the Joshua in you….

OUT TO IN MENTALITY

It is often in the way we look at things that will determine how long we stay in some things.

Have you ever been in a situation and thought more about how you got into it rather than how you can come out of it?

God will sometimes allow us to go through a place in order to get us to another place. Our problem is that we don't have the faith to leave one place and go to another. It may be because we have no hope or expectations that things will get better.

God does not take you from one place to another and the new place that He takes you is worse than the place that you left. That would not be an attribute of who God is.

Two things that always help me is that God is:

1- EL-SHADDAI- meaning the God who is **more** than enough.
2- PROVIDER- meaning He has **the provisions** that we need.

The term pro means to have a forward movement. God will move you forward by His nature. It is His command that we move forward in our lives. This is what He told Moses when Moses thought that he was in a bad place.

(Exodus 14:15 KJV) "And the LORD said unto Moses, Wherefore criest thou unto me? Speak unto the children of Israel, that they go forward:"

It has already been ordained for us to move forward in every area of our lives. WE need to trust that God has already been and is where He is taking us.

You can never go into a greater thing unless you are willing to come out from where you are.

Often the biggest obstacle to advancement is not people or circumstances. It is our own fear.

Fear will keep you where you are and never send you where you need to go. Fear will keep you stuck; faith will release you to more.

In Genesis, the story of Abraham, we see that God told Abraham to get out of his father's house and his father's country. Then God told him to go to a place that I will show you. Abraham had to believe God in order to do what God had commanded him to do.

The interesting thing about all of this is God's command came with a promise. He promised that if YOU get out, I WILL show you something that is already prepared.

Abraham never would have come into his greatness and the promise of God if he had stayed in a place called "Haran". It means –crossroads or place of decision.

Haran was where God called upon Abraham to make a decision. We all have a "Haran" in our lives. It is not by design that we stay at that place. It is by design that we make our decision at that place and move on into what God has in store for us.

The plan for Abraham was not in Haran. It was in the place where God would show him. God has a plan for all of us. It is not in the place of your own decisions. It is in the place that He is leading you. You have to trust Him that He has already been where He wants you to go. And that place is going to be better than where you are now. Go with his plan this time. You have gone long enough with your own plan. His plan is better than you can ever imagine for your life.

It has already been thought out for you. You have to now walk in what God has already thought out for your life.

(Jeremiah 29:11 KJV) "For I know the thoughts that I think toward you, saith the LORD, thoughts of peace, and not of evil, to give you an expected end."

Your coming out is closer than you think. Your going in (The Blessing) is closer than you know.

It is called "DECISION".

WILL TO SEPARATE

A will is defined as: *the power of making a reasoned choice or decision or controlling one's own actions.*

(2 Corinthians 6:17 KJV) "Wherefore come out from among them, and be ye separate, saith the Lord, and touch not the unclean thing; and I will receive you"

You have to be willing to identify the **"them"** in your life and have the <u>**will**</u> to separate yourself from **"them"**.

This is a must in order to make your life better today than yesterday.

When you start to separate yourself, the process allows you to look into your circumstance from an outward perspective. You will have a different perspective and that will yield you a different view on your life and on what you see.

Your will to do just that will allow you to see things as they are and give you a clearer view on whatever it is that you are dealing with. Perspective is just another way of saying that I am willing to look at this from another angle and maybe I will see something that I did not see before.

If you are willing to be honest with yourself, half of the battle is already won.

If you are willing to be honest with yourself, you will see that there is a **NEED** in your life to **separate** in order to get better.

Just as oil and water will not mix, you have to understand that joy and sorrow does not mix. **Positive and Negative** does not mix. Good and evil does not mix. Hope and Despair does not mix. All of these examples are of the type of things that repel each other. They are all contrary one to the other. In that same mind set you have to understand that sometimes in relationships things don't mix. Separating will not feel good but, it becomes a necessary part of your life and your life's process of **YOU** getting better.

If you understand the concept of no mix, you can apply it to situations and people in your life who have the opportunity to get better but refuse to get better. You have a decision to make at that point. Do you want to become as the Lepers of II Kings? Are you willing to sit (or stay) in life where you are? Are you willing not to allow anyone else to cause you to remain where you are and die. There is an old song that we used to sing all of the time in church. "If you don't want to go, then don't hinder me. I am determined that "I" am not going to allow anyone to hinder me from reaching my goal and purpose in life.

What say you? Don't just read it in this book.... Say it out loud!!!!!

Now start doing it with everything that is within you.

A will is designed to express your wishes. You need to express your will to have more, to do more, to be more, to see more. Then do whatever it takes to make your life better today than yesterday and get released.

Will it to yourself!! Not just to someone else. Let it first be in you.

(2 Corinthians 8:12 KJV) "For if there be first a willing mind, it is accepted according to that a man hath, and not according to that he hath not."

Start today and write the will of your heart by the way you respond to the negative thoughts and words that come your way. Remember that wills are formed and expressed by one's own actions.

Say it today!! Do it today!! *I will separate myself from everything and everybody that does not line up with the thought that I am in the process of getting and doing better and in the process of release.*

Now that you have done that! There is only one thing left to do:

Identify and Separate Yourself by your Will.

HEALING POWER OF THE WORD

We have all heard the saying, "sticks and stones will break bones but words will never hurt you". We know from experience that this not a true statement. I want to take a quick look at how you can handle the "words" that do hurt.

We can never in this age that we are living or in the past, stop words from coming after us.

They are coming whether we like it or not. Life will sometimes issue you things that you did not ask for or sign up for.

The question is not the issues. The question is how you are going to respond to life and issues that you didn't ask for?

One of the greatest secrets in life is that no matter how much damage the words did. You can be healed from the damage that they caused.

You may not have caused the hurt but you can do something about how long the hurt hangs around you.

I believe that this is one of the greatest revelations of all times.

(Psalm 107:20 KJV) *"**He sent his word, and healed them, and delivered them from their destructions.**"*

As I was reading this, the Spirit of God revealed this to me and it helped me.

Notice what it says. **"He sent His word"**, God sent Word to them. It does not say that He sent his word to heal them or for their healing. All it says is that God sent His word and what God sent healed those that were injured.

If God had sent His word for healing only, then the Word of God could not be effective in your life in other areas. Whatever God sent, (His Word) became healing for those who were in need of healing.

That is why the Word of God is so powerful. It is limitless in our lives if we allow it to be.

God's word can heal, if we allow it to heal us.

God's word can encourage, if we allow it to encourage us.

God's word can deliver, if we allow it to deliver us.

God's word can console, if we allow it to console us.

And because it is not limited to just healing notice what it says. That same word that **healed** also **delivered**.

A deliverer- _meaning to take away_, it took them away from destruction.

God loves us so much that if we can start to accept His word over everything else, the Word will become everything that is missing in our life.

So now the question becomes, what do you need in your life?

Then whatever you need, the Word of God can come in and address your needs.

In the natural, the sweetest love song that you can think of is comprised of words. It is the meditation on those words that will start to work for you.

The Word of God is the greatest love song that you can have; it will not work for you until you start to meditate in it and let it work on you.

All you have to do is allow God access into your heart and let Him work out the details of handling your needs

ARE YOU HERE TO DEMOTE OR PROMOTE

No matter how many people are in your life or around you, they are there for a reason.

You can put people in two categories of life. They will be in your life to **promote** you and what God has placed on the inside of you or they are there to attempt to **demote** you from your assignment.

Promote will build you up.

Demotion can only take you down.

It is not hard to figure out. Look at what happen to Peter on the Sea of Galilee.

He was in a boat with people that he was supposed to be in a relationship with.

But when Peter decided to do something that nobody had done before, Peter had no support from the boat people.

You have to recognize that you are on an assignment and need to know who is with you in your boat.

If the people, who are in the boat with you, are not speaking the same language that you are, then they are not really with you.

You have to get to the point that when your life depends on everything that you believe that you are called to, you have to be willing to say to people around you; **"If you are not in this with me to promote what I am doing and where I believe God is taking me, Then get out of my boat"!**

Every one of them in the boat had the same opportunity in life.

But only Peter believed God enough to step in a direction that he had not gone before.

ARE YOU FIT FOR THE ASSIGNMENT

HE that puts his hand to the plow and looks back is not fit for the kingdom.

(Luke 9:62 KJV) And Jesus said unto him, No man, having put his hand to the plow, and looking back, is fit for the kingdom of God.

THE ENITRE POINT OF YOUR LIFE AND MINE

IS THAT GOD GETS THE GLORY

It is like you going into a department store and trying on a new outfit.

For what purpose do you try on a new outfit?

IT IS A FIT TEST when people that you used to hang with suddenly come back into your life.

GOD IS ALLOWING us to see whether or not that old stuff still fits or not.

IT IS NOT UNTIL YOU BECOME UNFIT FOR WORLDLY THINGS THAT YOU BECOME FIT FOR THE KINGDOM.

Find out whether or not that old talk still fits.

Find out whether or not that old life style still suits you.
Find out whether or not the stuff that you used to drink stills satisfies.

You have to be willing to tell others what does not fit into your life anymore.

Why an un-Godly life style no longer fit.

Why unholy conversations no longer fit.

Why old mind sets no longer fit.

Why the seventeen works of the flesh no longer fit.

And why the nine components of the Spirit do work.

It is because you are now fit for the Kingdom

What you are drinking and walking in and living in now has to prove to be stronger than what we used to allow and accept in our lives.

(Romans 8:1 KJV) *"There is therefore now no condemnation to them which are in Christ Jesus, who walk not after the flesh, but after the Spirit."*

<u>MEANING THAT YOUR NOW HAS TO BE DIFFERENT FROM YOUR THEN</u>

This is not about your house or your car. It is about your life and the assignment that God has given you.

It is not enough to tell others what things you are no longer fit for. We have to be bold enough to tell them what we have been "outfitted" to do.

The above passage starts by telling us that God is looking for those who are willing not to look back.

Only those who refuse to look back are fit according to the Scripture. Looking back means to consider what's behind you over what's in front of you.

I know that we all have memories. Our memories should not be the guiding force in our life.

Looking back will always mess up your focus.

We have to understand the difference between "looking back" and a "flashback".

<u>Looking back</u> is what Lot's wife did in Genesis 19, and because she considered the things behind her more important than the assignment in front of her. She became unfit for the forward movement of God in her life and generations of people were hurt by her decision.
(Those connected to her)

A <u>flashback</u> is a momentary look back into the history of what you left. Flashbacks will come without provocation. A flashback can only become a look back if you dwell on it. Flashbacks can leave just as fast as they come by the reception that they receive.

A little bit of advice*:* ***Flashbacks wear dresses and put make-up on. Flashbacks wear suits and animal print shoes***.

Now that you know that, what kind of reception are you going to give your "Flashbacks"? Need help? Flash them back to where they came from.

If one woman's decision to look back affected a generation, tell me what will happen to those connected to you in your generation if you refuse to look back.

So go ahead, get ready to try on some new stuff that God has ordained for you. That is why that old stuff does not satisfy you anymore. You need to understand that your taste has changed.

(Psalms 34:8 KJV) O taste and see that the LORD is good: blessed is the man that trusteth in him.

FINAL WORD

Finally we come to the close of this subject for now.

I hope that you can remember that God has the final word in everything.

Ecclesiastes 12:13

Let us hear the conclusion of the whole matter: Fear God, and keep his commandments: for this is the whole duty of man.

(Eph 6:10 KJV) Finally, my brethren, be strong in the Lord, and in the power of his might.

God released you to do His work. He first had to release you from the bondage of sin.

Look at this :

(1 John 1:9 KJV) If we confess our sins, he is faithful and just to forgive us our sins, and to cleanse us from all unrighteousness.

If you have understood in an earlier chapter about <u>Free is Free</u>. Then you should understand that **ALL is ALL.**

God comes into our lives and cleans us from ALL un-right things. (Unrighteousness)

Not some but all.

(Heb 8:12 KJV) For I will be merciful to their unrighteousness, and their sins and their iniquities will I remember no more.

So when God sets you free, He does not send you out to be paroled.

When you are paroled, you still have things hanging over your life. That is the way of men and not the way of God.

God does not want you to remember the things in your life that He forgot. So why would you remember what God said, He would not ?

Let that sink in for a moment.

The reason that you can serve Him now is because your record has been expunged and there is no record that you had committed the crime.

So, you may say how can I be freed and not paroled? Follow this simple but powerful formula and watch God move on your behalf.

(Isa 55:6 KJV) Seek ye the LORD while he may be found, call ye upon him while he is near:

(Isa 55:7 KJV) Let the wicked forsake his way, and the unrighteous man his thoughts: and let him return unto the LORD, and he will have mercy upon him; and to our God, for he will <u>abundantly pardon.</u>

At the end of the day, when the jury comes back with a verdict on your life.

God still has the final word.

God has in His awesome plan already laid out for you an escape clause to every situation in your life.

The enemy has already shown up and made an accusation against you and the will of God in your life. You just need to know one thing when the enemy accuses you,

You have already been sustained by God!

When he says you are no good,

God says sustained!

When he says they don't deserve your Mercy and Grace,
God says sustained!

When the enemy says that it is time for you to give up,

God says sustained!

When the enemy says that you are not going to make it,
God says sustained!

In our court system, when an objection is made by the adversary, the Judge will render his decision based on the objection.

When the Judge "sustains" an objection, he is really saying "I have heard what you said but the witness does not have to answer to it."

(Hebrews 12:2 KJV) "Looking unto Jesus the author and finisher of our faith; who for the joy that was set before him endured the cross, despising the shame, and is set down at the right hand of the throne of God."

Why is God saying sustained in every area of your life that the enemy is attempting to destroy and defame you?

It is because of who is standing in your corner speaking for you.

(1 John 2:1 KJV) "My little children, these things write I unto you, that ye sin not. And if any man sin, we have an <u>advocate with the Father</u>, Jesus Christ the righteous:"

(1 John 2:2 KJV) "And he is the propitiation for our sins: and not for ours only, but also for the sins of the whole world."

In everything that we were accused of, God sent his son to answer for us.

He answered to every penalty with His blood on the cross.

He paid the cost with His blood and because He paid it all,

You can be sustained.

This does not mean we were not guilty, He took the blame for it and that is what made everyone who accepts what He did   FREE….

(Revelation 21:6 KJV) *"And he said unto me, It is done. I am Alpha and Omega, the beginning and the end. I will give unto him that is athirst of the fountain of the water of life freely."*

Amen, to God be the Glory.

You are set free from your past.

You are no longer bound by your past and no longer a prisoner.

You are now released from **Yesterday!**

Bethel Covenant Worship Center
3958-F Wrightsboro Road
Augusta, GA 30909

Pastor Reginald Bynes
And
First Lady Cynthia Bynes